curiousabout

MILITARY
ROBOTS

BY LELA NARGI

AMICUS LEARNING

What are you

curious about?

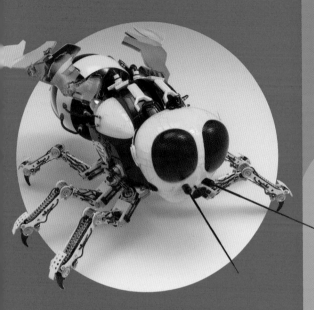

CHAPTER THREE
3

Military Robots of the Future
PAGE
14

Curious about is published by
Amicus Learning, an imprint of Amicus
P.O. Box 227
Mankato, MN 56002
www.amicuspublishing.us

Editor: Rebecca Glaser
Series and Book Designer: Kathleen Petelinsek
Photo Researcher: Omay Ayres

Library of Congress Cataloging-in-Publication Data
Names: Nargi, Lela, author.
Title: Curious about military robots / by Lela Nargi.
Description: Mankato, MN : Amicus Learning, 2024. | Series:
Curious about robotics | Includes bibliographical references and
index. | Audience: Ages 5-9 | Audience: Grades 2-3 | Summary:
"Questions and answers give kids an understanding about the
technology of military robots, including how the military uses
robots and what makes them unique. Includes infographics to
support visual learning and back matter to support research
skills, plus a glossary and index"– Provided by publisher.
Identifiers: LCCN 2023013270 (print) | LCCN 2023013271
(ebook) | ISBN 9781645496533 (library binding) | ISBN
9781681529424 (paperback) | ISBN 9781645496793 (pdf)
Subjects: LCSH: Military robots–Juvenile literature.
| Armed Forces–Robots–Juvenile literature.
Classification: LCC UG450 .N374 2024 (print) | LCC UG450
(ebook) | DDC 629.8/92–dc23/eng/20230524
LC record available at https://lccn.loc.gov/2023013270
LC ebook record available at https://lccn.loc.gov/2023013271

Photo credits: Alamy/WENN Rights Ltd, 12; AP Images/
SOPA Images, 7; Dreamstime/Nerthuz, cover, 1; Shutterstock/
Gorodenkoff, 2, 10, Josh McCann, 3, 14; MikeDotta, 2, 6;
sdecoret, 16–17; shrimpgraphic, 10t; SugaBom86, 11; Stanford
University/Biomimetics and Dexterous Manipulation Laboratory,
7; Teledyne Flir/Black Hornet® PRS, 7; U.S. Air Force/Airman 1st
Class Collin Schmidt, 8, Airman 1st Class Shannon Moorehead,
11b; U.S. Army/General Dynamics Land Systems, 11, Historical,
19; U.S. Marines Corps/Lance Cpl. Julien Rodarte, 10b, 12–13,
20, Lance Cpl. Ryan Kennelly, 5, Lance Cpl. Yuritzy Gomez, 15,
Lance Cpl. Jennifer E. Reyes, 18; U.S. Navy/John F. Williams,
7, Mass Communication Specialist 1st Class Brian A. Goyak, 9

Printed in China

How does the military use robots?

Men and women in the military have risky jobs. Robots make their jobs safer. Robots fight in battles. They can find hurt people. They clear **mines** and fight fires. **Drones** peek at the action up ahead.

A U.S. marine learns to use a drone during a training exercise.

What do military robots look like?

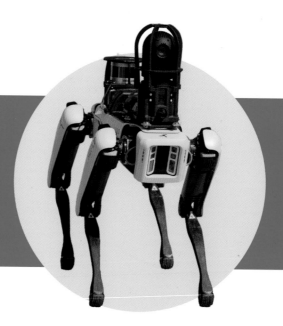

A robot "dog" can search for danger.

They are all different. One robot is a tiny dumbbell. Others are shaped like dogs or humans or bugs. Some are whole tanks or airplanes. The GuardBot is round and rolls over water or land. Some are top secret. **Civilians** have no idea what they do or how they look.

PD100 BLACK HORNET
A TINY HELICOPTER USED AS A SPY ROBOT

STICKYBOT
THIS BUG-SHAPED ROBOT CAN CLIMB STRAIGHT UP A WALL!

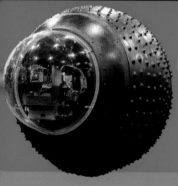

GuardBot
ROLLS ACROSS SAND OR EVEN WATER TO SPY, GUARD, OR RESCUE.

MUTT
HALF TANK, HALF TRUCK, MUTT HELPS CARRY GEAR FOR SOLDIERS.

SAFFiR
A HUMANOID ROBOT THAT FIGHTS FIRES ON NAVY SHIPS

CHAPTER TWO

What special features do military robots need?

The Grizzly robot can travel across rough land.

It depends on what they do. CRACUNS was built to never rust. This robot launches from the sea to spy from the air. The Grizzly robot has tracks on its wheels. It carries heavy tools over rough land for soldiers. The TALON robot has arms for different jobs. It also has **sensors** that work in the dark.

Soldiers can stay a safe distance away when the TALON robot checks on devices that could explode.

Small spy drones fly using rotors, like a helicopter.

How do they move?

Tracks let this military robot move easily across land.

Large spy drones fly with no pilots on board.

Robots with tracks can move across bumpy land. Robots with legs are quiet and quick. Flying spy robots need **rotors** or wings. Some robots can do missions on their own. They are **autonomous**. Soldiers use remote control for other robots.

A robot dog can walk on four legs.

How do military robots know what to do?

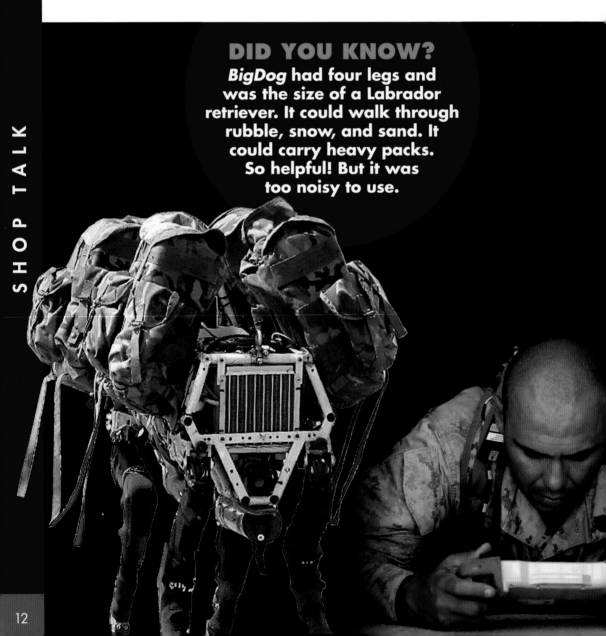

DID YOU KNOW?
BigDog had four legs and was the size of a Labrador retriever. It could walk through rubble, snow, and sand. It could carry heavy packs. So helpful! But it was too noisy to use.

Like all robots, they have a computer brain. It is filled with **code** that tells them what to do. Map a danger zone. Find a target. Show people to safety. Search through rubble. People program robots to do these jobs.

Two marines look for nearby threats using a robot with a camera.

CHAPTER THREE

MILITARY ROBOTS OF THE FUTURE

Will military robots get better?

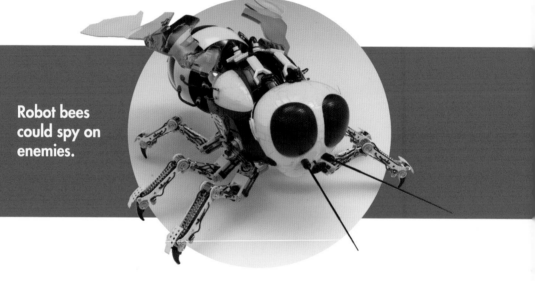

Robot bees could spy on enemies.

Scientists are working on it. What if you could wear a robot, like Iron Man? An **exoskeleton** would make you extra strong and fast. Want to spy better on people talking? Robot bees are in the works. Some folks hope for giant battle robots. We will see!

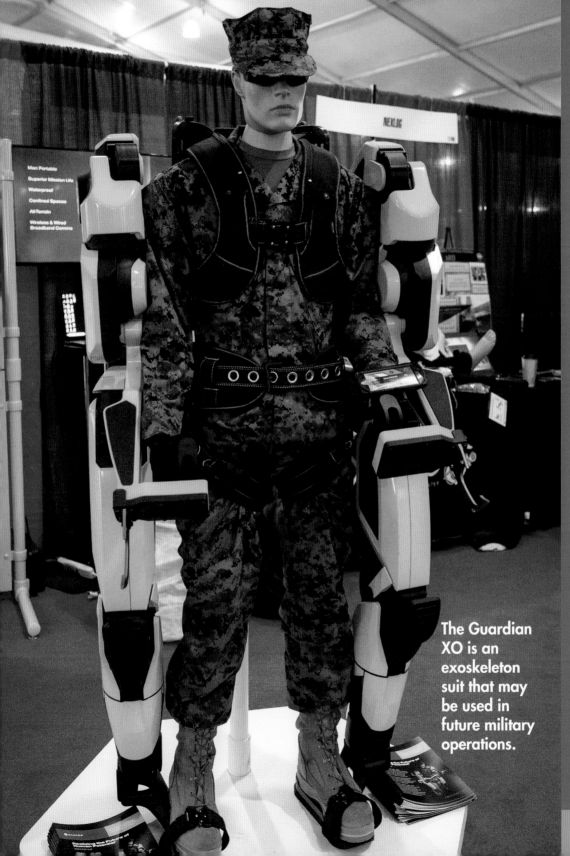

The Guardian XO is an exoskeleton suit that may be used in future military operations.

Will robots get smarter?

Artificial intelligence
may help robots
become smarter.

Scientists are working on that too. AI stands for **artificial intelligence** (AI). Robot brains with AI learn on their own. Is it safe to land here? Are guns nearby? Where should we drive our tank? AI will help robots learn these things.

The U.S. Marines use robot targets for training.

Will we ever have robot soldiers?

DID YOU KNOW?
The first military robots
were 5-foot (1.5-m) tanks.
They were used in
World War II to
find mines.

British soldiers
captured these
German tanks during
World War II.

Yes. They are here. The military is testing many now
and soon there will be more. Some already train
human soldiers. Some are getting ready for war.
They do not feel pain. They do not mind heat or
cold. They are hard to push over.

Why does the military want to use robot soldiers?

Human soldiers can get hurt or die. They stay safer if robots fight instead. But some people think robot soldiers are a bad idea. They ask questions such as: Do we want robots to pick who is friend or foe? What do you think?

The U.S. Marines are testing the "dragon fire" robot, which can work day or night. Using robots for dangerous tasks can keep soldiers safer.

ASK MORE QUESTIONS

Can I build my own robot spy?

How do drones work?

Try a BIG QUESTION: Will robots take too many jobs from people?

SEARCH FOR ANSWERS

Search the library catalog or the Internet.
A librarian, teacher, or parent can help you.

Using Keywords
Find the looking glass.

Keywords are the most important words in your question.

?

If you want to know about:

- building a spy robot, type: BUILD SPY ROBOT KIDS

- flying drones, type: HOW TO FLY DRONES

FIND GOOD SOURCES

Are the sources reliable?

Some sources are better than others. An adult can help you. Here are some good, safe sources.

Books

Military Robots in Action
by Mari Bolte, 2024.

Robots All Around Us: From Medicine to the Military
by Emmett Martin, 2023.

Internet Sites

Atlas Gets a Grip
https://www.youtube.com/watch?v=e1_QhJ1EhQ
Watch the humanoid robot Atlas, created by Boston Dynamics, lift, climb, and jump just like a human.

GuardBot Media
https://guardbot.org/media/
Watch how this round robot can roll through snow, sand, grass, or water on its missions!

Every effort has been made to ensure that these websites are appropriate for children. However, because of the nature of the Internet, it is impossible to guarantee that these sites will remain active indefinitely or that their contents will not be altered.

SHARE AND TAKE ACTION

What ways do you think military robots can help?

Could they help kids stay safe? Could they show us secret hiding spots?

Military robots, pro or con?

Make a list of good and bad things about robot soldiers. Should they fight instead of humans? Will they take over the world?

Design your own robot.

What should a military robot be able to do? How many arms will it need? How many tools and sensors?

GLOSSARY

artificial intelligence A computer tool that lets robots learn on their own.

autonomous Acting on its own without help.

civilian A person who is not a soldier.

code A set of instructions that humans write into computers.

drone A flying robot that can "see" and take pictures.

exoskeleton A robotic suit worn on the outside of the body.

mine A piece of metal on land or in the ocean that explodes when you touch or step on it.

rotors Spinning blades like on top of a helicopter that make a craft fly.

sensor Something that detects light, movement, or sound and responds to it.

INDEX

About the Author

Lela Nargi is a journalist and the author of 25 science books for kids. She's a long-time sci-fi fan who has always wondered what it would be like to have a useful robot in the house. What tasks would she most want it to do? Making the bed, definitely. For now, she lives in New York City with a dachshund named Bigs who has probably never wondered about robots at all.